CORE LIBRARY OF US STATES

Connecticut

BY AUDREY HARRISON

CONTENT CONSULTANT
Erin Kuprewicz, PhD
Natural History Engagement Specialist/Collections Manager, Connecticut State Museum of Natural History, Institute of the Environment; Manager of Vertebrate Collections, Biodiversity Research Collections, Department of Ecology and Evolutionary Biology, University of Connecticut

Core Library
An Imprint of Abdo Publishing
abdobooks.com

abdobooks.com

Published by Abdo Publishing, a division of ABDO, PO Box 398166, Minneapolis, Minnesota 55439.

Printed in the United States of America, North Mankato, Minnesota.
052022
092022

Cover Photo: Shutterstock Images
Interior Photos: Denis Tangney Jr./iStockphoto, 4–5, 10–11, 45; Red Line Editorial, 7 (Connecticut), 7 (USA); Miro Vrlik/Zuma Press/Newscom, 12–13, 43; Comet Design/Shutterstock Images, 17 (flag); Shane Gross/Shutterstock Images, 17 (whale); Wilfred Marissen/Shutterstock Images, 17 (robin); Melinda Fawver/Shutterstock Images, 17 (flowers); Tatyana Sanina/Shutterstock Images, 17 (mantis); Alexander Farnsworth/iStockphoto, 20–21; Romiana Lee/Shutterstock Images, 23; Brian E. Kishner/Shutterstock Images, 25; Jeff Holcombe/Shutterstock Images, 28–29; Gabe Palmer/Alamy, 31; Alanson Fisher/National Portrait Gallery/Smithsonian Institution, 34–35; S. M. Garten/Shutterstock Images, 38

Editor: Marie Pearson
Series Designer: Joshua Olson

Library of Congress Control Number: 2021951387

Publisher's Cataloging-in-Publication Data

Names: Harrison, Audrey, author.
Title: Connecticut / by Audrey Harrison
Description: Minneapolis, Minnesota : Abdo Publishing, 2023 | Series: Core library of US states | Includes online resources and index.
Identifiers: ISBN 9781532197482 (lib. bdg.) | ISBN 9781098270247 (ebook)
Subjects: LCSH: U.S. states--Juvenile literature. | Northeastern States--Juvenile literature. | Connecticut--History--Juvenile literature. | Physical geography--United States--Juvenile literature.
Classification: DDC 974.6--dc23

Population demographics broken down by race and ethnicity come from the 2019 census estimate. Population totals come from the 2020 census.

CONTENTS

CHAPTER ONE

THE CONSTITUTION STATE

Families hop aboard a steam train. The train will take them to see some of Connecticut's most beautiful sights. With the sound of the train's whistle, the ride starts. They peer eagerly out the windows. The fall colors on the trees outside are brilliant shades of red and orange. They see geese flying to a nearby lake. The train passes through historic towns including Deep River. The town has existed since the 1600s. The tourists can't wait to explore

New Haven, Connecticut, gets its peak fall colors in early to mid-November each year.

PERSPECTIVES

THE CHARTER OAK

When Connecticut was a British colony, it had a charter that gave it the right to create its own government. The British later tried to establish more control of the colony by taking the charter away. A man named Joseph Wadsworth is often credited for hiding the charter from the British. He hid it in an oak tree that was later named the Charter Oak. This tree became a symbol of US independence from Great Britain. It fell down and was destroyed in a storm on August 21, 1856. But the Charter Oak remains an important symbol of Connecticut's identity. The Charter Oak is the state tree of Connecticut. It appears on quarters celebrating the state.

more of the natural sites and rich history that Connecticut has to offer.

ABOUT CONNECTICUT

Connecticut is the southernmost of the six New England states. This region is in the northeast corner of the United States. The region was named by English settlers who arrived there in the 1600s. Connecticut is bordered by New York to the west. Massachusetts lies to the north. Rhode Island

MAP OF CONNECTICUT

Take a close look at some of the cities in Connecticut. What do you notice about where they are in relation to bodies of water? Why might these locations be important?

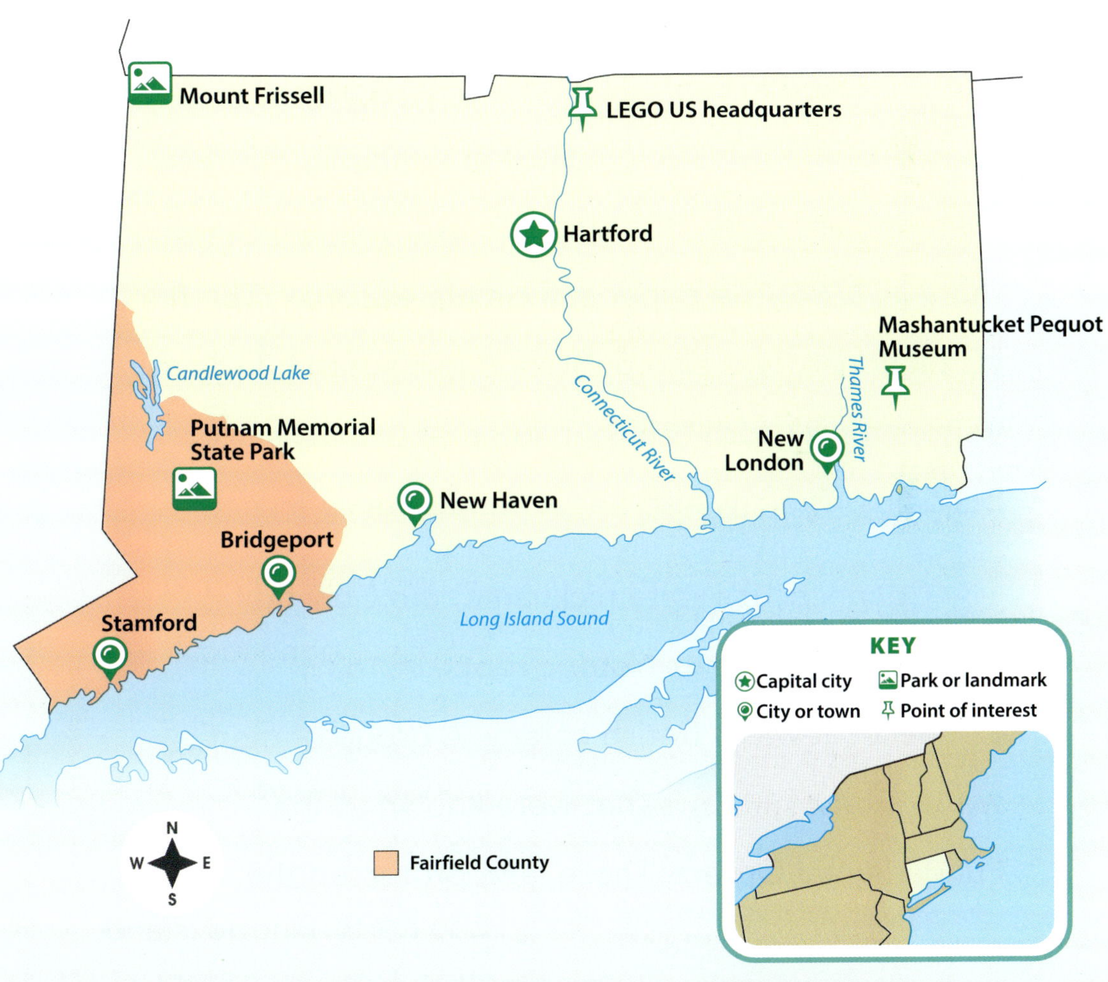

is to the east. Connecticut's southern border is on Long Island Sound. This body of water connects to the Atlantic Ocean. Connecticut is one of the smallest states by area. It is divided into just eight counties. Yet more than 3 million people live there.

Connecticut's biggest cities are scattered throughout the state. Hartford is the capital city and is located in central Connecticut. Hartford is known for many historic firsts. For example, the first US newspaper, the *Hartford Courant*, was published there in 1764. The paper still circulates today. The first US dictionary was also published in Hartford. Today visitors to Hartford can tour some of the city's historic buildings. The city also has art and science museums.

Connecticut's state nickname, the Constitution State, comes from its historic roots. In 1639 Connecticut was a British colony. A group of men wrote a list of 11 laws that were known as the Fundamental Orders. These laws protected the rights of Connecticut residents. By 1787 the United States had won its independence from Great Britain. Government leaders wrote the US Constitution, which helped establish the US government and protect the rights of citizens. The US Constitution was partly inspired by Connecticut's Fundamental Orders. This is how Connecticut got its nickname.

Fairfield County is located in southwestern Connecticut. It stretches toward New York City. It includes cities such as Stamford and Bridgeport. Fairfield connects outdoor activities

YALE UNIVERSITY

Yale University was founded in Connecticut in 1701. It is one of the oldest and most highly esteemed universities in the United States. Yale moved to New Haven in 1716, where it still runs today. In 1802 Benjamin Silliman taught a chemistry course at Yale. This is considered to be the first modern science course taught in the United States. The university's library houses more than 15 million books. Five US presidents have attended the school, including William Howard Taft and the Bushes.

Stamford lies on Long Island Sound. Around 129,000 people live in the city.

with city life. People can hike and visit Connecticut's Beardsley Zoo. Or they can eat dinner in Stamford and see a show at the Palace Theatre.

Connecticut is also home to many small towns that often have a town center. That's where the parks,

churches, town hall, schools, and some stores are located. People live along the roads leading out of the town center. Connecticut shows off its history in exciting ways. With a blend of quaint towns and historic cities, the state has something for everyone.

CHAPTER TWO

HISTORY OF CONNECTICUT

Paleo-Indians lived in the Connecticut region starting at least 12,500 years ago. The Paleo-Indians were skilled workers. Their villages were near rivers and streams. They fished and hunted large animals and also gathered plants for food. They made stone tools to help them hunt.

By the 1600s Algonquian-speaking peoples dominated the region. There were between 5,000 and 7,000 people split among several nations in 1614. They farmed corn,

People of the Mashantucket Pequot Tribal Nation continue to celebrate their culture today.

AN ALGONQUIAN NAME

Connecticut's state name comes from the Mohegan language. This language is part of the Algonquian language family. The Mohegans called the area *Quinnehtukqut*, which translates to "long river place" or "beside the long tidal river." No one speaks fluent Mohegan today. The last fluent speaker, Fidelia Fielding, died in 1908. But her great-great grandniece Stephanie Fielding has been studying the language. She is working to create a Mohegan dictionary and grammar book to restore her people's language.

beans, squash, and tobacco. They hunted local animals. Pequot people lived near the Thames River. They were closely connected to their Mohegan neighbors. The same sachem, or chief, ruled both groups until the early 1600s. Then they split apart. In the north-central and northeastern areas of what is now Connecticut, Nipmuc people lived in villages. Each village had its own sachem. People in the villages would occasionally ally with the Mohegans and other nearby peoples.

COLONIAL HISTORY

European settlers came to Connecticut from Massachusetts in the 1600s. The first European settlement in Connecticut was established in 1633 in present-day Hartford. The Pequot were friendly with the settlers at first. But relations grew tense as more and more British settlers came. Struggles began when white settlers took over Pequot land. The Pequot War of 1637 lasted 11 months. British troops attacked the Pequot and burned down their homes. Hundreds of Pequot died. Most survivors fled to areas that are now parts of other states. Some joined nearby American Indian nations.

The Mohegans took in many Pequot. They made a deal with the British, hoping to keep their land. But European settlements interfered with their way of life. Because of this, many Mohegans moved away. Additionally, European diseases killed many American Indians. By the end of the 1600s, the Nipmucs were likewise losing land to white settlers. Some Nipmucs joined Europeans and took up the Christian religion. Others moved west or to Canada.

European settlers cleared forests on the land. They built homes. They farmed and traded goods. But space for farmland was limited. So they soon changed to manufacturing goods in factories instead. These factories helped make weapons and supplies during the Revolutionary War (1775–1783).

INDEPENDENCE AND STATEHOOD

During the Revolutionary War, Connecticut and the other American colonies fought Great Britain. They wanted to be an independent nation. The colonies won the war. Connecticut became the fifth US state on January 9, 1788.

Connecticut's state government has three branches. An assembly makes laws in the legislative branch. The assembly is made up of 36 senators and 151 representatives. The governor leads the executive branch. The judicial branch is the court system.

CONNECTICUT
QUICK FACTS

Connecticut is unique in many ways. How does the information in this graphic help you better understand the state?

Abbreviation: CT
Nickname: The Constitution State
Motto: *Qui transtulit sustinet* (He who transplanted still sustains)
Date of statehood: January 9, 1788
Capital: Hartford
Population: 3,605,944
Area: 5,543 square miles (14,356 sq km)

STATE SYMBOLS

State animal
Sperm whale

State flower
Mountain laurel

State bird
American robin

State insect
European mantis

PERSPECTIVES

FOSSIL DISCOVERY

On August 23, 1966, Edward McCarthy, a bulldozer operator, was excavating a site in Rocky Hill for a new highway. He turned over a slab of gray sandstone and was surprised to see three huge footprints with three toes embedded into the rock. These footprints ended up being the tracks of a dinosaur known as *Eubrontes giganteus*. After McCarthy's discovery, workers uncovered about 2,000 more tracks. Many people wanted to see the tracks preserved, so the highway's path was moved away from the site. Connecticut officials created Dinosaur State Park to preserve these fossils, and *Eubrontes giganteus* was named the state fossil in 1991.

At first many of Connecticut's towns were located near fertile valleys and fishing coasts. But as the state's economy became more industrial, people began moving to cities where factories were located. The population boomed in the mid-1800s. In 1850 manufacturing was Connecticut's largest industry.

In 1943 the Connecticut government established the

Inter-Racial Commission. This group worked to ensure that people of all races had equal employment opportunities. It was the first of its kind in the United States. At this time Black Americans and other people of color were treated poorly throughout the United States. Often the only jobs available had low wages or harsh working conditions. Connecticut continues to address racial discrimination. The state has a rich history with diverse cultures that make Connecticut what it is today.

EXPLORE ONLINE

Chapter Two discusses Connecticut's independence from Great Britain. The website below talks about Connecticut's role in the Revolutionary War in greater detail. Does it answer any questions you had about the war?

CONNECTICUT IN THE REVOLUTIONARY WAR

abdocorelibrary.com/connecticut

CHAPTER THREE

GEOGRAPHY AND CLIMATE

Connecticut's landscape is made up of rolling hills and valleys. The Berkshire Hills are located on the western side of the state. This is a part of the Appalachian Mountains. Connecticut's highest point is located in the Berkshire Hills along the slope of Mount Frissell. Mount Frissell's peak is in Massachusetts. But the side that is in Connecticut reaches 2,380 feet (725 m) high. The hills are covered in hardwood forests. Birch, beech, and maple trees grow there.

The Berkshire Hills have many hiking opportunities for people to explore.

Lakes can be found throughout the state. Candlewood Lake is in the western region. It is the largest lake in Connecticut.

The eastern region of the state is also hilly. Many rivers, including the Thames River, run through this region. The Thames River flows into Long Island Sound. The river's fresh water mixes with salt water from the Atlantic Ocean in the sound. The sound provides important habitats for many types of animals, including fish and birds. Long Island Sound attracts fishermen who come looking for oysters and lobsters.

OYSTERS

Oysters are marine animals. They live in shallow ocean waters around the world. An oyster's strong muscles keep its hard shell closed for protection. Inside rests a soft, slimy body. Many people enjoy eating oysters for their salty taste. Oysters also contain some healthy nutrients, such as iron and calcium. Connecticut is known for its oysters. Farms there produce more than 200,000 bushels (7,000 cubic m) of oysters each year.

The Connecticut River has cultural and historical significance. In 1998 it was named an American Heritage River.

Rivers also run through the flatter central region of the state. The Connecticut River is the longest river in New England. It runs for 410 miles (660 km) through four states, starting in New Hampshire and flowing south. It cuts Connecticut in half and empties into Long Island Sound. In addition, sandstone and shale building materials are mined in the central part of the state.

Approximately 60 percent of Connecticut is forested. More of the land used to be forested. But it was cleared for agriculture. The loss of forests is a loss of habitat for wildlife, especially big animals. Bears and wolves were common hundreds of years ago. Without their forest habitats, most died out or moved away. Wild turkeys also died out in Connecticut in the 1900s. But people successfully brought them back to the area. The turkey population was stable by 1981.

Deer, racoons, and beavers live throughout the state. The mountain laurel is native to Connecticut. This is the state flower of Connecticut. Its pink-and-white petals stand out in dark green forests. Shorebirds such as the American oystercatcher live on the coast. And American robins often nest in Connecticut throughout the winter. They shelter in evergreen trees and eat berries. The American robin is Connecticut's state bird.

WEATHER AND CLIMATE

Connecticut's weather is mild. This means it rarely gets above 90 degrees Fahrenheit (32°C) or below 0 degrees Fahrenheit (−18°C). Rain falls fairly consistently throughout the year. On average Connecticut receives

American oystercatchers look for oysters and clams hiding in stony and sandy spots along the water.

44 to 48 inches (112–122 cm) of rain each year. This helps with farming.

The weather in Connecticut can change quickly. The state experiences some extreme weather. Thunderstorms and tornadoes can occur near the Connecticut River. Hurricanes may land in Connecticut. These storms cause wind damage and can lead to flooding. The deadliest hurricane to reach Connecticut happened in 1938. It had wind speeds of more than 74 miles per hour (119 km/h). Nearly 700 people died. More than 60,000 people lost their homes.

PERSPECTIVES

NORTHEASTERS

In December 2020 Connecticut experienced its first northeaster of that winter season. Some parts of the state received as much as 9 inches (23 cm) of snow. The heavy snow caused power outages. Tree branches fell onto roads after snapping under the weight of the snow. People living in Connecticut know they have to be prepared for extreme changes in weather, especially during the winter. William Robles was in Bolton, Connecticut, when the snowfall began. He said, "You have to be prepared because the weather can change on you real fast."

Blizzards are common in some parts of Connecticut. They are known as northeasters or nor'easters. The northwestern hills get the most snowfall in the state. It is common for 75 inches (190 cm) of snow to fall in this part of the state in a year. Other areas of Connecticut average 35 to 45 inches (90–115 cm) of snow each year.

STRAIGHT TO THE SOURCE

Hurricane Sandy, also known as Superstorm Sandy, hit Connecticut on October 29, 2012. It was one of the most damaging hurricanes in US history. Connecticut government officials reflected on the hurricane five years later. In a press release, Department of Housing commissioner Evonne M. Klein said:

> *Superstorm Sandy will go down in history as one of the most destructive natural disasters to ever hit our state. . . . Under the steadfast leadership of Governor [Dannel] Malloy, Connecticut was able to return to "normal" as quickly and as safely as possible. As the state continues to rebuild, we are doing so with the understanding that another storm of this magnitude could hit Connecticut again.*

Source: "Gov. Malloy: Five Years after Superstorm Sandy, Connecticut Has Made Significant Storm Resiliency Improvements." *Office of Governor Dannel P. Malloy—Archive*, 31 Oct. 2017, portal.ct.gov. Accessed 9 Feb. 2021.

WHAT'S THE BIG IDEA?

Take a close look at this passage. What is being said about Superstorm Sandy? What does it tell you about the role of the government during natural disasters?

CHAPTER FOUR

RESOURCES AND ECONOMY

In the 1600s mining was an important part of Connecticut's economy. The land contained iron and copper. Raw materials such as gravel and sand are still mined in the state today. But many of the original mines are now closed.

Agriculture plays a small part in Connecticut's economy. Milk, eggs, chicken, and tobacco are the biggest agricultural products. Seafood is another source of money for the state. Most of this money comes

Some companies in Connecticut, such as Suzio York Hill, still mine for materials used to make asphalt, concrete, and crushed stone.

WHALING

Whaling was banned in the United States in 1971. But whaling was once an important part of Connecticut's economy. One of the world's largest whale ports was located in New London. This port brought in $1 million in 1850 alone. That is worth more than $31 million today. People once used whale blubber for oil and candles. But overhunting led to a decline in whale numbers. The industry suffered as a result. Connecticut's last whaling trip ended in 1909. In honor of its whaling history, Connecticut named the sperm whale as its state animal in 1975.

from Connecticut's oyster industry. This industry alone brings in $8 million each year.

MANUFACTURING

Today manufacturing is the biggest industry in Connecticut. Manufacturing is tied to the state's history of invention. Some famous inventions from Connecticut include sewing machines, lollipops, and calculators. The steamboat, typewriter, and PEZ candy were also invented there. These products were made and sold by Connecticut businesses.

Companies hire skilled workers to install important parts on transportation equipment.

The variety of products made in Connecticut has changed over time. During World War II (1939–1945), Connecticut factories made weapons and defense supplies for the rest of the country. In the 1970s technology companies grew. Today metal, plastic, and electronic products are some of the most common items manufactured in the state. Transportation equipment is another major focus. These products include jet engines, helicopters, and more.

Connecticut's location near Massachusetts and New York gives people many job options.

PERSPECTIVES

COMMUTING TO NEW YORK CITY

Approximately 43,000 people commuted from Connecticut to New York City for work in 2017. Many took the train to work. Over the years, Connecticut residents have seen an increase in the amount of time this commute takes. Some old tracks can no longer be used, making the commute less efficient. Connecticut governor Ned Lamont proposed a plan to improve the commute. He said, "New York is the global capital of the world right now. We're part of that metropolitan center. . . . So, shame on us if we push us further and further away from all the jobs and the opportunity there."

They can live in Connecticut but work in other states. Still, many businesses have offices in Connecticut. The US headquarters for LEGO is in Enfield. Financial jobs make up a large part of the local economy. In the 2010s, more than 100 insurance companies were located in the state. Hartford is sometimes called the Insurance Capital of the World because of the many insurance companies there.

FURTHER EVIDENCE

Chapter Four discusses Connecticut's history of manufacturing and invention. What was one of the main points of this chapter? What evidence is included to support this point? Read the article at the website below. Does the information on the website support the main point of the chapter? Does it present new evidence?

ECONOMY

abdocorelibrary.com/connecticut

CHAPTER FIVE

PEOPLE AND PLACES

Many famous people in American history have come from Connecticut. Harriet Beecher Stowe is one of Connecticut's most famous writers. She was born in Litchfield in 1811. She is most well-known for writing the novel *Uncle Tom's Cabin*, which showed her antislavery beliefs. Her Hartford home is now a museum. People can visit to learn more about her life and writing.

Harriet Beecher Stowe's novel *Uncle Tom's Cabin* was very popular. In the first year after it was published, it sold around 300,000 copies.

European influence is apparent in Connecticut. The Wadsworth Atheneum Art Museum is known for its collection of European art. It is the oldest operating museum in the United States. In addition, many of Connecticut's towns are named after places in England.

Connecticut's nonwhite populations grew in the 2000s. The Latino population is the fastest-growing ethnic group in the state. Latino people in the state have roots in countries throughout Latin America. In 2013 Carmen E. Espinosa became a justice

HELEN KELLER

Helen Keller was born in Alabama in 1880. She became sick when she was 19 months old. She recovered from the illness but lost her sight and hearing. Growing up, she was frustrated that she couldn't communicate with others. Then her teacher Anne Sullivan helped her learn to spell with her fingers. Keller became dedicated to her education. She eventually learned to speak. Then she used her voice to advocate for people with disabilities. Keller spent the last 32 years of her life in Easton, Connecticut. She was inducted into the Connecticut Women's Hall of Fame in 2006.

for the Connecticut Supreme Court. She was the first person of Latin-American heritage in this role. Yale University also hosts a yearly film festival that is dedicated to Latino, Spanish, and Portuguese filmmakers.

There are two federally recognized American Indian nations in Connecticut. They are the Mashantucket Pequot Tribal Nation and the Mohegan Tribe. The Connecticut state government recognizes three other nations. These are the Eastern Pequot Tribal Nation, the Golden Hill Paugussett, and the Schaghticoke Tribal Nation.

The Mashantucket Pequot Museum teaches people about northeastern American Indian histories and cultures. It has a large collection of historical information and artifacts. Historians can use these materials for research. The museum also hosts a yearly art market and works to highlight American Indian voices today.

Some people enjoy seeing the beautiful old houses in Wethersfield.

Nearly 17 percent of Connecticut's population is Hispanic or Latino. And more than 12 percent is Black. In the past some enslaved people escaped the South and headed to the North. Many Black people built their own communities in the state, such as Little Liberia in Bridgeport. Today Connecticut's Black voters work with government leaders to help improve life in Black communities.

Connecticut also has a variety of fairs and carnivals that occur throughout the state. These events usually happen in the summer and fall. People enjoy food, live music, petting zoos, agricultural exhibitions, and more.

FAMOUS PLACES

Connecticut's rich history attracts many tourists. They can visit the Museum of Connecticut History in Hartford. They can see colonial homes in Wethersfield. Other historical sites include Putnam Memorial State Park. It celebrates Israel Putnam, who was an American general during the Revolutionary War.

PERSPECTIVES

CONNECTICUT STATE PARKS

Connecticut's state parks are the main draw for tourism in the state. Approximately 10 million people visit the state parks every year. Since 2018 Connecticut residents who have registered their vehicles in the state are able to enjoy these parks for free. Visitors can hike and explore the outdoors through extensive trail systems. Others choose to pay a fee to camp in the state parks. In 2019 Governor Ned Lamont reminded Connecticut residents of the beautiful views that are close to home. He said, "I encourage all Connecticut residents—and visitors to our great state—to explore the many outdoor recreation opportunities this state has to offer."

The Mystic Seaport Museum includes a re-creation of a seaport village from the 1800s. Museum visitors can also see fishing ships from this time period.

Connecticut has sites for those who enjoy the outdoors. People can explore the state's 32 state forests and 110 state parks. Connecticut's location on Long Island Sound means there are plenty of sandy beaches for swimming and fishing. Bridgeport and Stamford are two of Connecticut's more populated cities. Both are located on the sound. People can also enjoy the beaches of inland lakes.

Yale University in New Haven is another draw to the state. The school consistently ranks as one of the best in the country. Beyond the classroom, Yale is home to art galleries and museums too.

Connecticut is a small state with a lot to offer. Its rich history combines with modern businesses. From beautiful beaches to bustling cities, Connecticut has something for everyone.

STRAIGHT TO THE SOURCE

Connecticut tourism expanded in the 2010s. The Connecticut Office of Tourism encourages people to explore the state. In the fall of 2020, the department released a press statement that said:

> *With the longest fall foliage season in New England, and one of the most colorful in the world, Connecticut is poised to provide an unbeatable backdrop for months of seasonal fun—closer to home. From scenic drives through rolling hills and outdoor adventures by land or sea, to culinary delights on the farm and overnight getaways and camping, Connecticut provides a convenient fall getaway destination filled with both beloved and brand-new autumn experiences and events . . . at every turn.*

Source: "Connecticut Announces Fall Foliage Forecast and Seasonal Experiences." *PR Newswire*, 2 Sept. 2020, prnewswire.com. Accessed 26 Mar. 2021.

BACK IT UP

The author of this passage is using evidence to support a point. Write a paragraph describing the point the author is making. Then write down two or three pieces of evidence the author uses to make the point.

IMPORTANT DATES

12,500 years ago

Paleo-Indians live in the Connecticut area at this time if not earlier.

1633

The first European settlement is built in Connecticut.

1639

A group of men in Connecticut writes the Fundamental Orders.

1788

Connecticut becomes the fifth US state on January 9.

mid-1800s

More people arrive in Connecticut as industrial jobs become more common.

1943

Connecticut forms the Inter-Racial Commission, the first of its kind in the United States.

2010s

More than 100 insurance companies have offices in Connecticut.

2012

Hurricane Sandy hits Connecticut on October 29.

STOP AND THINK

Tell the Tale

Chapter Three of this book discusses northeasters. Imagine you are experiencing a blizzard. Write 200 words about what you see and feel. What did you do to prepare for the snowstorm?

Surprise Me

Chapter Four discusses the history of manufacturing and inventions in Connecticut. After reading this book, what two or three facts about industry did you find most surprising? Write a few sentences about each fact. Why did you find each fact surprising?

Say What?

Studying states can mean learning a lot of new vocabulary. Find five words in this book you've never heard before. Use a dictionary to find out what they mean. Then write the meanings in your own words and use each word in a new sentence.

Another View

This book talks about Connecticut's geography. As you know, every source is different. Ask a librarian or another adult to help you find another source about this topic. Write a short essay comparing and contrasting the new source's point of view with that of this book's author. What is the point of view of each author? How are they similar and why? How are they different and why?

GLOSSARY

advocate
to defend or speak about a cause

charter
a document that guarantees certain rights and freedoms

discrimination
when people treat others differently based on certain factors such as appearance

federal
having to do with the national government

fertile
rich in nutrients for growing plants

foliage
plant leaves

habitat
the place where a plant or an animal lives

insurance company
a type of business that financially protects a person's health or belongings

magnitude
of great size or power

sound
a body of water between two larger bodies of water or between an island and the mainland

ONLINE RESOURCES

To learn more about Connecticut, visit our free resource websites below.

Visit **abdocorelibrary.com** or scan this QR code for free Common Core resources for teachers and students, including vetted activities, multimedia, and booklinks, for deeper subject comprehension.

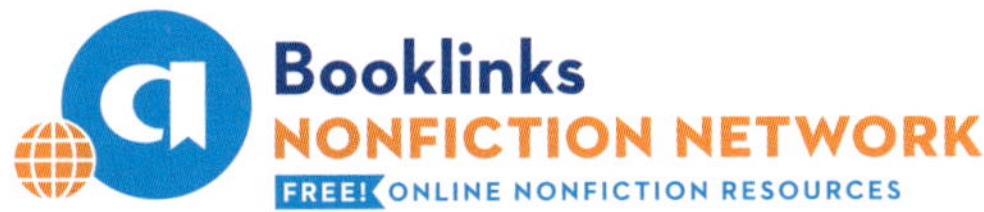

Visit **abdobooklinks.com** or scan this QR code for free additional online weblinks for further learning. These links are routinely monitored and updated to provide the most current information available.

LEARN MORE

Gagne, Tammy. *Fact and Fiction of American Colonization*. Abdo, 2022.

Hamilton, John. *Connecticut*. Abdo, 2017.

Miller, Derek, et al. *Connecticut*. Cavendish Square, 2020.

About the Author

Audrey Harrison lives in Minnesota. She enjoys mystery novels and jigsaw puzzles. She has been to 18 US states and hopes to visit many more!